Folding the Starburst Sections

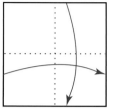

1. Fold into quarters.

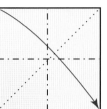
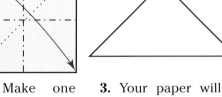

2. Make one diagonal fold.

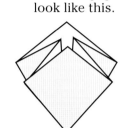

3. Your paper will look like this.

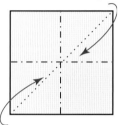

4. Unfold triangle and collapse sides inward.

5. Fold up. Repeat 1-5 to make 4 sections.

INSTRUCTIONS:
Fold 5 Polka Dot 3" x 3" paper pieces referring to diagrams above. Edge both sides of all sheets with Red ink. Adhere the folded sheets together by adhering square panels end to end. Be sure to use the panel that does not have a fold. • Cut Red ribbon in half. Adhere a piece of ribbon diagonally across each end piece. Adhere 1½" x 1½" Pink cardstock pieces to each end over ribbon. Edge Pink cardstock with Red ink. • Journal on the outer panels of Polka Dot paper with Red marker. Punch small hearts from Red cardstock and adhere next to journaling. • Flatten Red bottle cap. Adhere to front cover. Punch 1" round Pink cardstock, edge with Red ink and adhere to bottle cap. Punch a small Red heart. Adhere to bottle cap. Cut letters from Cutable, edge with Red ink and adhere to bottle cap. Cover heart and letters with Glossy Accents for added dimension. Let dry. • String glass bead over both ribbons. Tie a Lark's Head knot and trim off excess ribbon. Slide bead to toward the cover's point to hold booklet in the closed or open position.

1. Fold into quarters.

2. Make one diagonal fold.

3. Fold up.

4. Adhere sections together.

A Starburst of Love
Mini Ornament

Create a miniature star book bursting with love and creativity.

MATERIALS:
Cardstock (Pink , Red) • Polka Dot Decorative paper • Cutables Letter Squares • 1 Red bottle cap • Glass bead • 16" of Red ⅛" satin ribbon • *Clearsnap* Scarlet Chalk ink • Red marker • Punches (1" round, small heart) • Bone folder • *Ranger* Glossy Accents • Adhesive

MATERIALS:
Cardstock Red (five 1½" x 1⅝", ⅜" x 7½") • Decorative paper (3" x 12", ¼" x 3") • Cutables Letter Squares • *Ranger* (Distress Ink Vintage Photo, Cut n' Dry Foam) • Adhesive • Small photos

Mini Accordion Folder Pattern

INSTRUCTIONS:
Accordion fold decorative cardstock to 3" x 3". Open and lay flat. Center template in each panel and trace. Cut and score each panel's template. Adhere a Red cardstock square to the center of each panel along with a small photo. Cut letters from Cutable and adhere to card. Add Vintage Photo ink to all four edges using Cut n' Dry Foam. Accordion fold first two sections on score lines. Reversing the direction, accordion fold the second two sections on score lines. To make band, place score lines at 3", 3¼", 6¼", and 6½". Fold and adhere overlap together. Adhere decorative strip of paper to band.

Captured Laughter
Mini Accordion Folder

Capture freeze-frames of a happy moment in this unique folding card.

  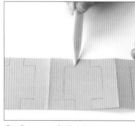  

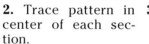 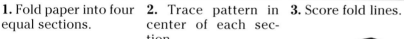

1. Fold paper into four equal sections.

2. Trace pattern in center of each section.

3. Score fold lines.

4. Cut rectangles.

5. Fold up card.

A box full of... Love

MATERIALS:
2½" x 3½" x 1½" paper mache box • Decorative papers (1 large dots 12" x 12", 1 small dots 12" x 12", 10 small dots 2" x 2¾") • Tags • Sticker numbers and alphabet • 12 Red bottle caps • Navy ⅛" satin ribbon • 12 Red ⅛" eyelets • 22" Navy zipper • Small photos • *Clearsnap* Midnight Blue Pigment Ink • Navy marker • ⅛" hole punch • Needle • Navy thread • Eyelet setter • Adhesive

1. Sew a stop at end of zipper.

2. Apply adhesive tape to outside edge of zipper.

3. Adhere zipper to inside of box lid.

4. Adhere zipper to outside of box bottom.

10 Reasons Why I Love You
Mini Zipper Box

Tell someone how much you love them with this zippered keepsake box... no sewing required.

INSTRUCTIONS:
Box: Cover box outside with decorative cardstock. Edge with Midnight Blue ink. Cut zipper to 14". Using needle and thread, sew a stop at zipper end. Open zipper and adhere to outside of box bottom. Adhere zipper to inside of box top. Cover inside of box with decorative paper. Decorate box top with tags and stickers.

Cards: Edge each card with Midnight Blue ink. Punch hole and set eyelet in top left corner of each card. Flatten bottle caps. Adhere a bottle cap to each card. Add a number sticker to each bottle cap. Decorate each card with tags and photos. Journal on each card with Navy marker. Tie all 10 cards together with Navy satin ribbon.

Itty Bitty Brag Book

A perfect purse or pocket size brag book that's sure to travel everywhere!

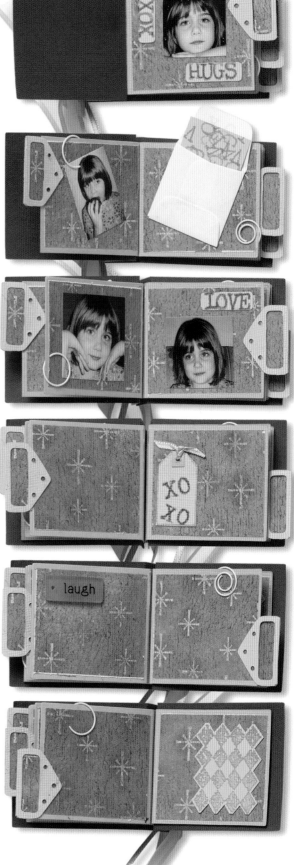

MATERIALS:
Cardstock 12" x 12" (Purple, Butter, Pink) • Decorative paper • *Creative Impressions* (Star eyelets, mini spiral paper clips) • *DMD* 1" mini envelope • Pink ribbons • Word charm • Small photos • *Clearsnap* Vivid Lavender ink • Stamps (*Stampendous* Alphabets, Diamonds, Tags) • *Sizzix* Dies (Triangle Tab, Mini Booklet) • *QuicKutz* Alphabet Dies • Punches (1" round, 1/16" hole) • Adhesive

INSTRUCTIONS:

Booklet: Die-cut mini book cover from Purple cardstock. Die-cut inside pages from Pink cardstock. Die-cut tabs and cut spine cover piece from Butter cardstock. Adhere spine piece to front cover. Set star eyelets. Assemble inside pages and covers. Tie with Pink ribbons. Adhere a 1 5/8" x 1 7/8" piece of decorative paper to each page. For each page, insert a 1/2" x 1" piece of decorative paper into tab and adhere tab to page.

Cover: Stamp Diamond design on Butter cardstock in Lavender ink. Trim. Adhere. Die-cut R from decorative paper. Stamp letters in Lavender ink, trim and adhere. Flatten bottle cap and adhere. Punch a 1" round photo and adhere to the bottle cap.

    Page 1: Stamp "XO's" and "Hugs" on Butter cardstock in Lavender ink. Adhere to page along with a photo. Attach paper clip.

    Page 2 & 3: Adhere photo to page. Adhere envelope to page. Stamp "XO" in Lavender ink. Stamp letters in Lavender ink all over a 1 1/8" x 1 1/4" piece of Butter cardstock and insert into envelope.

    Page 4 & 5: Adhere photos to pages. Stamp "Love" in Lavender ink on Butter cardstock. Adhere to page.

    Page 6 & 7: Stamp small tag on Butter cardstock in Lavender ink. Cut out. Cut a small piece of pink cardstock and adhere to top of tag. Punch a 1/16" hole and tie on pink ribbon. Adhere to page.

    Page 8 & 9: Adhere word charm. Attach paper clip.

    Page 10 & 11: Stamp Diamonds on Butter cardstock in Lavender. Trim and adhere to page.

1. Cut, fold and adhere strips together.

2. Ink edges.

3. Apply strip to bottom and each end for pocket.

4. Insert card into pocket.

Best Friends

A boy and his dog are together forever in this accordion style pocket album.

MATERIALS:

Ivory cardstock (3 of 2½" x 3½", 2 of ¼" x 12") • Toy Blocks paper • Cutables (Number Blocks, Color Words) • 3 Manila Mini Folders • Silver bottle caps • Silver wire clips • Photo tabs • *Ranger* (Distress Inks: Vintage Photo, Peeled Paint; Cut n' Dry Foam) • Black fine point marker • Stamps (*Stampendous* ABC's, *Stamprite* words) • Labeler • 1" Round punch • Rubber band • ¼" Red liner tape • Adhesive

INSTRUCTIONS:

Cut 2 strips 3" x 9" from Toy paper. Fold each in half and half again. Unfold and adhere end together to create one long strip. To create pocket, cut 2 strips 1½" x 9". Fold each in half and half again. Open and adhere end to end to create one long strip. Apply tape to bottom edge and each end. Attach strip. • **Pocket inserts:** Edge Ivory cardstock pieces with Peeled Paint ink using Cut n' Dry Foam. Add photos. Embellish with Cutable words. Add Silver clips. • **Inside:** Punch 1" round photos. Adhere to bottle caps. Adhere to panels. • Edge folders with Peeled Paint and Vintage Photo inks using Cut n' Dry Foam. Stamp words in Vintage Photo ink. Adhere Cutable words. Adhere folders to panels. Attach photo tabs with brads. Run ¼" wide strips of Ivory cardstock through labeler. Gently rub Peeled Paint and Vintage Photo inks using Cut n' Dry Foam over raised text. Adhere to pocket panels. • **Front:** Edge folder with Peeled Paint and Vintage Photo inks using Cut n' Dry Foam. Stamp words. Cut numbers from Cutables. Edge with Black ink. Adhere. Stamp letters on rubber band in Peeled Paint ink. Shadow letters with Black marker.

7

Mini Matchbook

Keep memories of journeys past sacred in this fabulous little matchbook album.

MATERIALS:
Traveler double-sided cardstock • Slide Mounts (Weathered Wood, Victorian) • Cutables (Letter Squares, Color Words, Wings & Things, Twenties Kids) • *Ranger* (Distress Inks: Vintage Photo, Black Soot, Antique Linen; Cut n' Dry Foam) • Small Brown bag • Sanding Block • Decorative Stapler • Paper towels • Adhesive

INSTRUCTIONS:
Cut a 3" x 9" piece of Traveler cardstock. Score at $3^7/8$" and $8^1/4$". Using Cut n' Dry Foam ink edges with Vintage Photo and Black Soot inks on both sides of paper. **Inside:** Tear off corner section of leftover Traveler paper. Create a burned look by coloring torn edge with Vintage Photo ink using Cut n' Dry Foam. Add a touch of Black Soot ink to edge with Cut n' Dry Foam. Glue to top right corner on inside. Tint edges of brown bag with Vintage Photo and Black Soot ink. Insert brown bag into bottom edge and staple. Cut card from trading card strip. Scratch surface with Scrappers Block. Ink surface with Antique Linen. Wipe off excess ink with paper towel. Scratch surface of Weathered Wood small slide mount. Cover surface with Vintage Photo ink. Wipe away excess ink. Cut two corners from slide mount and adhere to corners of trading card. **Outside:** Scratch surface of small Victorian slide mount. Cover with Vintage Photo ink. Wipe off excess ink. Color edges with Black Soot ink using Cut n' Dry Foam. Cut photo from Cutable strip. Adhere to back of slide mount. Adhere slide mount to front. Cut words and postcard from Cutable strips. Adhere to slide mount.

1. Tear edge of paper.

2. Color torn edge with Vintage Photo ink.

3. Add a touch of Black Soot ink.

4. Fold bottom edge up, insert brown bag, staple.

Visit us online: www.d-originals.com

1. Draw long measurement on plexiglass.

2. Score by cutting along line with blade.

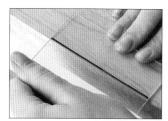

3. Holding firmly, lay on edge of table and break on score line.

4. Apply vaseline to center of plexiglass.

5. Paint entire surface. Let dry.

6. Wipe paint and vaseline off with a paper towel.

Mini Clipboards

Adhere magnets to the back of these miniature clipboards and add fun to your refrigerator door!

Laugh

MATERIALS:
Games paper • Salsa slide mounts • Cutables (Ransom Letters, Dark Words, Typewriter) • Silver metal clip • Star charm • *Ranger* (Distress Inks: Vintage Photo, Black Soot; Glossy Accents, Cut n' Dry Foam) • Sanding Block • Paper towel • Adhesive

INSTRUCTIONS:
Cut dark Typewriter Key section of Cutable to 3½" tall. Lightly sand surface. Cover with Vintage Photo ink. Wipe off excess ink with paper towel. Sand surface of slide mount. Cover with Vintage Photo ink. Wipe off excess ink with paper towel. Attach metal clip; adhere to card. Adhere photo to mount. Cut image from Games paper; adhere to bottom left edge of card. Cut word and dominoes from Cutables; adhere to mount. To add dimension, cover word, dominoes and game image with Glossy Accents. Let dry. Adhere star charm to metal clip.

Butterfly Love

MATERIALS:
Cardboard 2½" x 3½" • Flutterby Decorative paper (Lime Dots 2½" x 3½", Tiles flowers 1¾" x 2½") • Stickers (Flutterby Rounds, Postoids) • Pink metal clip • Cutables (Letter Squares, Light Words) • Plexiglass • *Clearsnap* Rouge Chalk ink • *Ranger* Glossy Accents • *Delta* acrylic paint (Turquoise, Ivory) • Vaseline • Paper towel • Adhesive

INSTRUCTIONS:
Paint cardboard Turquoise; let dry. Tear Dots edges. Edge with Rouge ink. Adhere to cardboard. Adhere flowers from Tiles paper over Dots. **Plexiglass:** Cut 1¼" x 2" plexiglass. Score with blade. Lay on table edge; break on score line. Repeat for second measurement. Apply vaseline to center. Apply Ivory over entire surface; let dry. Wipe Vaseline off using paper towel. Lightly brush Turquoise on edges. Place photo beneath. Attach clip; adhere to board. **Embellish:** Cut letters/words from Cutables. Edge with Rouge ink. Adhere to board and plexiglass. Cut butterflies from stickers; adhere to board. Cover embellishments with Glossy Accents. Let dry.

Senior '86

MATERIALS:
Cardboard 2½" x 3½" • Cardstock (2" x 3" Ivory, 1½" x 2⅜" Brown) • Cutables (Print Blocks, Typewriter, Letter Squares) • Black metal clip • *Ranger* (Distress Ink Vintage Photo, Glossy Accents, Cut n' Dry Foam) • *Delta* acrylic paint (Ivory, Burgundy) • Paper towel • Adhesive

INSTRUCTIONS:
Paint cardboard Burgundy; let dry. Brush edges with Ivory paint. Edge Ivory cardstock with Vintage Photo ink using Cut n' Dry Foam. Adhere to Cardboard. **Plexiglass:** Cut to 1¼" x 2". Apply vaseline to center. Apply Ivory over entire surface; let dry. Wipe Vaseline off with paper towel. Edge with Vintage Photo ink. Place photo beneath. Attach clip; adhere to board. **Embellish:** Cut letters, numbers, pencil and ruler from Cutable; adhere to board. Cover embellishments with Glossy Accents. Let dry.

Beach Buddies
by Adrienne Kennedy

Beach Buddies can be buddies forever.

MATERIALS:
Cardstock (Cream, Peach) • Green floral paper • Ivory buttons (2 medium, 1 large) • *My Sentiments Exactly* rubber stamps(Girl Friends, Vintage Calendar) • Tsukineko StazOn ink (Black, Teal) • Pastel fibers • Pearl strand • 2 Seashells • Adhesive

INSTRUCTIONS:
Adhere 7¾" x 7¾" Green floral paper to 8" x 8" Cream cardstock. Adhere 1" x 7¾" Peach cardstock to bottom of Green floral paper. On Peach cardstock squares, stamp BUDDIES in Black ink. Cut small tag and stamp Beach in Black ink. Adhere tag and letter squares to page. Stamp the date on the Peach strip and add accent stamps in Teal. Mat photo with Cream cardstock and adhere to page. Tie fibers and pearls onto page and secure in back. Adhere buttons and shells in place.

Cowboy Up
by Adrienne Kennedy

Place your Lil' Pardner's photo on this great layout.

MATERIALS:
Cardstock (Brown, White) • Decorative papers (Peach Paisley, Peach Stripes) • 3 Twine Strings 6¾" • 6 White Star brads • Ivory buttons (3 small, 1 large) • My Sentiments Exactly rubber stamps • Tsukineko StazOn Brown ink • Peach chalk • Adhesive

INSTRUCTIONS:
Adhere 6" x 7¾" Peach Paisley and 2" x 7¾" Peach Stripe to Brown 8" x 8" cardstock. Mat photo with Brown cardstock. Adhere to bottom right. Adhere 3 small buttons to bottom left. Adhere large button to top right corner. Adhere twine pieces to page. Attach star brad over each end of twine. In Brown ink on White cardstock pieces stamp "Cowboy" on 1¼" x 5¼", "Up" on 1¼" x 2¼", "Yee Haw" on 1¾" x 2¾". Color in letters with Peach chalk. Mat White cardstock with Peach Stripe paper. Adhere to page.

Girl Friends
by Adrienne Kennedy

Girls really do have fun with this charming scrapbook page.

MATERIALS: Orange Cardstock • Decorative papers (Green Diamonds, Pink Diamonds, Green Floral, Green Stripe, Pink Floral) • Metal tag • Checkered ribbon • Green fibers • Brads (Green, Red, Blue, Yellow, Light Green, Orange, Purple, Brass) • *My Sentiments Exactly* rubber stamps • *Tsukineko* StazOn Black ink • Adhesive

INSTRUCTIONS: Adhere 3⅞" x 7¾" Green Floral and 3" x 7¾" Stripe papers to Orange 8" x 8" square. Adhere 2½" x 7¾" Pink Diamonds paper ¾" from top of page. Stamp "Friends" in Black ink on Orange 1⅞" x 6¾" paper. Insert a brad into each letter's flower. Adhere over Pink Diamonds. Stamp "Girl" on Green Diamonds 1⅛" x 2½" paper. Adhere to corner of Friends piece. Tie ribbon and fiber around page. Tie tag to fiber. Adhere photo to Green Diamonds 2¾" x 4¼" paper. Adhere to page. Stamp Pocketful and Butterfly flower stamps in Black on Stripe paper. To make pocket, adhere 3¼" circles from Pink Floral and Pink Diamonds papers back to back. Fold sides toward center of circle. Insert brads. Wrap fibers around brads. Adhere to page. Stamp "Fun" over surface of Orange 1⅜" x 3" paper. Insert into pocket.

Snow Fun
by Adrienne Kennedy

Remember that fun, wintry day on this great page !

MATERIALS: Cardstock (Blue, White) • Decorative papers (Blue Circles, Printed vellum) • White tag • 4 Metal rimmed tags • Blue slide mount • 36" White ¼" organza ribbon • 2 Silver snowflake brads • White fibers • *My Sentiments Exactly* rubber stamps • *Tsukineko* inks (Brilliance Blue, Silver; StazOn Black) • Adhesive

INSTRUCTIONS: Adhere 7¾" x 7¾" Blue Circles paper to Blue 8" x 8" Blue cardstock. Adhere 5" x 5" printed Vellum to top left corner of Blue Circles. Mat photo with Blue cardstock. Attach snowflake brad. Adhere to top right. Fold 5" x 5" White cardstock and cut a snowflake. Tie white fibers around page. Adhere to page. Stamp "Fun" in Black ink on White cardstock and adhere to back of slide mount. Stamp small snowflakes in Silver ink on front of slide mount. Adhere to page. Stamp "Snow Fun" and snowflakes in Black ink on White tag. Stamp snowflakes in Blue and Silver on Tag background. Attach White ribbon. Attach snowflake brad. Adhere to page. Stamp word stamps in Blue ink on metal rimmed tags. Attach ribbon to each tag. Adhere tags to page.

Matchbox Mini Booklet

It's a match made in heaven when creativity and precious memories combine to make one very unique booklet.

MATERIALS:
Decorative paper (School Book Covers, Rulers) • Cutables (Print Blocks, Letter Squares, Typewriter) • Pen nib • Red wire clip • Red mini folder • Metal frame • Miniature puzzle pieces • Red window index tab • *Ranger* (Glossy Accents, Distress Ink Black Soot, Cut n' Dry foam) • ¼" hole punch • Adhesive

INSTRUCTIONS:
Cut two horizontal strips from School Book Covers paper. Adhere strips back to back. Accordion fold. Edge all sides with Black Soot ink using Cut n' Dry foam. **Panel 1:** Cut letters, pencil and ruler from Print Blocks Cutable and adhere. Cover letters with Glossy Accents. Let dry. **Panel 2:** Cut postcard, map and word from Letter Squares Cutable and adhere. Cover word with Glossy Accents. Let dry. Adhere pen nib. **Panel 3:** Edge Red mini folder with Black Soot ink. Adhere. Punch light typewriter keys from Typewriter Cutable using ¼" hole punch. Adhere typewriter keys and puzzle pieces to mini folder. Cover with Glossy Accents. Let dry. **Panel 4:** Attach Red wire clip. **Panel 5:** Cut ruler from Ruler paper. Insert into tab. Adhere to panel. Cut word from Letter Squares Cutable and adhere to tab. Adhere metal frame to panel. Fill with Glossy Accents. Let dry.

1. Adhere paper strips back to back.

2. Ink edges.

3. Accordion fold paper strips.

4. Apply Glossy Accents.

MATERIALS:
Thick chipboard (five 3½" x 3½", eight ¼" x 3½", four ¼"x 2⅞") • Cardstock (Tan 8" x 8", eight 2⅜" x 2⅜"; four Green 2⅞" x 3⅜") • Decorative paper (Soldier Green, Desert Courage) • Stickers (Dog Tag Alphabet, Armed Forces) • *Clearsnap* Colorbox Sepia Black pigment ink • 8 Silver ⅛" eyelets • Eyelet setter • ⅛" hole punch • X-acto knife • Adhesive

INSTRUCTIONS:

Box: See photos below. Adhere two long and one short cardboard strip to four 3½" x 3½" cardboard squares. Stack and adhere each layer alternately. Adhere fifth 3½" x 3½" cardboard square to top. Cover top and bottom with 3½" x 3½" Soldier Green paper. Cover all 4 sides with ¾" x 3½" Soldier Green paper. Cut where slits are with an X-acto knife.

Box top and bottom: Decorate with stickers and a photo. Color all edges with Sepia Black ink. **Inserts:** Cut 4 tabs from Tan cardstock using pattern. Line up tab on short side of 4 Green 2⅞" x 3⅜" cardstock pieces. Mark and punch holes with ⅛" hole punch. Print out tab titles. Make sure a title is printed for both sides of each tab. Insert titles between folded tab. Adhere tabs to Green cardstock pieces. Set two silver eyelets on each tab. Cut 8 Desert Courage 2¾" x 2¾" squares and adhere to both sides of each insert. Cut 8 Tan 2⅜" x 2⅜" squares and edge with Sepia Black ink. Adhere over Desert Courage square on both sides of each insert. Adhere a photo over Tan square on both sides of each insert. Slide inserts into box slits.

Tab Pattern

1. Cut cardboard pieces.

2. Adhere strips to squares.

3. Stack layers with openings in alternating directions.

4. Adhere chipboard top to box.

Flip-Flop Album Box

A one-of-a kind box houses images of a one-of-a-kind hero.

Jacob's Ladder
with Postale Papers
by Susan Charles

This themed trick ladder is a novel toy for any holiday.

HALLOWEEN MATERIALS:
12 squares thick chipboard 3" x 3" • Halloween Tiles paper • Ribbon (two Black 36", Green 36") • Adhesive

CHRISTMAS MATERIALS:
12 squares thick chipboard 3" x 3" • Christmas Tiles paper • Ribbon (3 Green 36") • Adhesive

INSTRUCTIONS:

1. Cut Tiles paper into 12 individual tiles. Adhere a tile on to each chipboard square. Lay tiles out into two rows of six (see diagram). Images on Row 1 should face the opposite direction of Row 2.

2. Turn Tile A from Row 1 face down. Adhere one end of each Black ribbon across top and bottom of tile with long ends to the right. Adhere one end of Green ribbon across center with the long end to the left.

3. Adhere Tile A from Row 2 on top. Make sure image is facing the correct direction.

4. Lay both Black ribbons over the tile going to the left. Lay the Green ribbon over the tile going to the right. Do NOT adhere the ribbon.

5. Stack Tile B from Row 1 face down on top. Make sure image is facing correct direction.

6. Lay Black ribbons over tile going to the right and adhere. Lay Green ribbon over the tile going to the left and adhere.

7. Stack and adhere Tile B from Row 2 on top. Continue alternating Steps 2-7 until all tiles have been used. Trim off excess ribbon at end.

Jacob's Ladder Diagrams

Row 2 | A B C D E F
Row 1 | A B C D E F

1. Cut Tiles paper into 12 tiles and adhere a tile onto each of the 12 chipboard squares.

2. Turn 1A over and attach ribbon to back of chipboard.

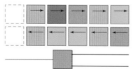

3. Attach 2A piece to top.

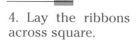

4. Lay the ribbons across square.

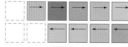

5. Stack 1B print side down.

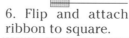

6. Flip and attach ribbon to square.

7. Attach 2B print side up to top.

MATERIALS:
Cardstock (12" x12" Ivory, Scraps of White, Red, Orange, Yellow, Blue) • Stickers (Red ABC's, Blue ABC's) • Bottle caps (Aqua, Red, Yellow) • Red metal clip • 2⅜" metal disk • Mini Manila file folders • Blue Magic Mesh • Red raffia • *Ranger* (Adirondack Rainbow Dye Ink Wildflower, Adirondack acrylic paint stream, Rubber brayer) • *Clearsnap* (Jumbo Rollograph, Botanical Tiles wheel, Aqua ink cartridge, Colorbox Chalk ink Prussian Blue) • X-acto knife • Bone folder • Punches (Large tag, 2" round, ⅛" hole) • Adhesive

INSTRUCTIONS:
Cut Ivory cardstock into 4 strips of 3" x 12". Load Wildflower ink onto brayer. Roll ink onto strips on one side. Continue to brayer on ink until strips are colored solid. Fold strip in half and open. Fold each outer edge to center fold to form a "gate" fold. Crease all folds with a bone folder. Repeat on all strips. • See diagram. To create pockets cut a horizontal, vertical or diagonal slit on alternating panels. • See diagram. Adhere panels shut, making sure to leave an area without adhesive for the pocket panels. Repeat process on all strips. Color all edges on both sides with Prussian Blue ink. Collate all 4 pages together and bind with Red raffia.

Front cover: Paint metal disk with Stream paint. Let dry. Punch a 2" Yellow cardstock circle. Adhere to metal disk. Cut letters "ME" from Red ABC's stickers and apply to disk. On a computer typeset "Book" and "About." Print out in Red, trim and adhere to disk. Flatten Yellow bottle cap, attach Red "A" sticker and Red metal clip. Adhere bottle cap to disk. **Inside:** Cut strips of Magic Mesh and apply to a few pages in book. Roll out Botanical Tiles Rollagraph images onto White cardstock in Aqua ink. Cut tiles and adhere to book pages. Flatten bottle caps, attach an ABC sticker and adhere to page. Edge mini folder with Prussian Blue ink and insert into pocket. Punch tags from Yellow and Red cardstock. Insert into pocket. Cut a 2" x 2" square from Blue cardstock. Punch a ⅛" hole in one corner. Insert card into pocket.

A Book About Me
Take time to fill this mini book with information and photos about who you are and what you do.

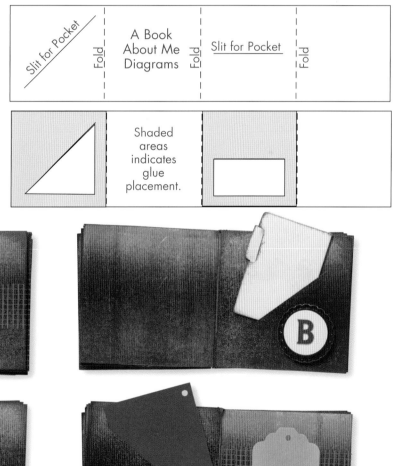

Mini Album Booklets
with Postale Papers

Keep a basket full of these darling mini albums in your living room and share your memories with guests when they come to visit.

BASIC INSTRUCTIONS:
Cut Tiles paper into 4 horizontal strips of 3" x 12". Fold strip in half and open. Fold each outer edge to center fold to form a "gate" fold. Crease all folds with a bone folder. Repeat on all strips.
To create pockets cut a horizontal, vertical, circular or diagonal slit on alternating panels. Also cut around images to create pockets. Adhere panels shut, making sure to leave an area without adhesive for the pocket panels.

Fall-tastic

Capture Autumn's splendor with this fun mini booklet.

MATERIALS:
Cardstock (Light Blue, Green) • Decorative papers (Coming Home Collection: 2 Tiles, Mosaic, Plaid, Stripes, Orange Leaves) • Stickers (Coming Home: Postoid, Round; Blue Words) • Bottle caps (1 Brass, 3 Green) • 36" Gold organza ribbon • Twill tape (Light Green, Brown with text • Mini Kraft file folder • *Clearsnap* Colorbox Brown pigment ink • Stapler • 1/8" hole punch • Adhesive

Trick or Treat

All treats and no tricks.

MATERIALS:
2 Halloween Tiles paper • Ribbon (18" Black, 6" Green, 6" Orange) • 1/8" hole punch • Adhesive

1. Fold strip in half and open.

2. "Gate" fold by folding outer edges to center.

3. Create pockets by cutting around images.

Merry Kissmas

A holly jolly creation.

MATERIALS:
2 Christmas Tiles paper • Ribbon (18" Red, 18" Green) • 1/8" hole punch • Adhesive

Hugs and Kisses

Express your love.

MATERIALS:
Decorative paper (Love Collection: 2 Tiles, Mosaic) • 36" Pink Organza Ribbon • Wire clips (Pink, 2 White) • *Clearsnap* Colorbox Brown pigment ink • 1/8" hole punch • Adhesive

Flutterby

Spring has sprung.

MATERIALS:
Flutterby Tiles paper • Ribbon (36" Green polka dot, 18" Pink satin, 2" Stripe) • Stickers (Flutterby Rounds, Postoids; Pink Words) • White mini file folder • Pink bottle cap • 3 Pink wire clips • Pink marker • *Clearsnap* Colorbox pigment ink (Light Blue, Pink) • 1/8" hole punch • Adhesive

Spoiled Cat

Show off your furry friend.

MATERIALS:
Decorative papers (Pet Collection: Tiles, Stripes) • Stickers (Pet Postoid, Black Words) • Black bottle cap • Ribbon (18" Black, 12" Black polka dot) • Black metal clip • 3 Red wire clips • Mini file folders (Red, Black, White) • *Clearsnap* Colorbox Sepia Black pigment ink • Punches (1/8" hole, 1" round) • Adhesive

Michele Charles

One of the most effervescent, exciting, and effective teachers of multi-media in the industry today is Design Originals' senior educator, Michele Charles. Michele travels across the country bringing her energetic presentation style and sense of humor to workshops that are loaded with innovative technique. Her classes are fun-filled excursions designed to ignite the creativity of everyone she meets. This versatile artist dedicates herself to developing fresh project ideas for rubber stamping, cardmaking, scrapbooking, altered art, trading cards, calligraphy and polymer clay. For more information, visit Michele's website at www.michelecharles.com

SUPPLIERS - Most craft and variety stores carry an excellent assortment of supplies. If you need something special, ask your local store to contact the following companies:

DECORATIVE PAPERS, CARDSTOCK, BOTTLE CAPS, STICKERS, CUTABLE STRIPS, METAL CLIPS
   Design Originals, 817-877-0067, Fort Worth, TX
INKS, RUBBER BRAYER, CUT N' DRY FOAM & NIBS
   Ranger Industries, 800-244-2211, Tinton Falls, NJ
DAUBER, INKS
   Tsukineko, 800-769-6633, Redmond, WA
PALETTE STAMP & STICK GLUE PAD
   Stewart Superior, 800-558-2875, San Leandro, CA
MAGICSTAMP PENSCORE, STAMP POSITIONER, ROLLAGRAPH, INKS
   Clearsnap, 888-448-4862, Anacortes, WA
PRISMACOLOR PENCILS
   Sanford, 800-323-0749, Bellwood, IL
MINI CRAFT IRON
   Clover, www.clover-usa.com
RUBBER STAMPS
   A Stamp In the Hand, 310-884-9700, Carson, CA
   Eclectic Omnibus, 602-564-0133, Glendale, AZ
   Hero Arts, 800-822-HERO, Emeryville, CA
   Impression Obsession, 877-259-0905, Williamsburg, VA
   JudiKins, 310-515-1115, Gardena, CA
   Magenta, 450-922-5253, Ste. Jolie, Quebec, Canada
   My Sentiments Exactly, 719-260-6001, Colorado Springs, CO
   Posh Impressions, 800-421-7674, Lake Forest, CA
   River City Rubberworks, 877-735-2276, Wichita, KS
   Stampendous, 800-869-0474, Anaheim, CA
   Stampers Anonymous, 800-945-3980, Cleveland, OH
   Stampington, 877-782-6737, Laguna Hills, CA

MANY THANKS to my friends for their cheerful help and wonderful ideas!
Kathy McMillan • Jennifer Laughlin
Patty Williams • Donna Kinsey
David & Donna Thomason

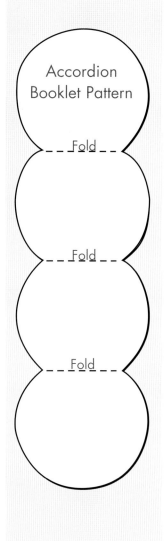

Accordion Booklet Pattern

_ _ _ Fold _ _ _

_ _ _ Fold _ _ _

_ _ _ Fold _ _ _

Bottle Cap Booklet
Mini Card

Get bitten by the love bug with this easy-to-make, pocket-size card with miniature accordion booklet.

MATERIALS:
Pink Cardstock • Polka Dot paper • Stickers (Pink Words, Flutterby Rounds) • 2 Lime Green bottle caps • Adhesive
INSTRUCTIONS:
Adhere 2¼" x 2¼" Polka Dot paper to 2½" x 2½" Pink cardstock. Adhere 1½" x 1½" Pink square over Polka Dot paper on its point. • Cut accordion booklet pattern from Polka Dot paper. Attach Word and Flutterby Rounds stickers. Fold up accordion style. Adhere a bottle cap to each end. Place a Flutterby Rounds sticker on front cover. Adhere bottle cap booklet to card.